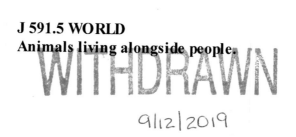

ANIMALS AT WORK

Animals
Living Alongside People

WORLD
BOOK

World Book, Inc.
180 North LaSalle Street
Suite 900
Chicago, Illinois 60601
USA

Produced for World Book, Inc. by Bailey Publishing Associates Ltd.

For information about other World Book publications, visit our website at **www.worldbook.com** or call **1-800-WORLDBK (967-5325).**

Library of Congress Cataloging-in-Publication data has been applied for.

Title: Animals Living Alongside People
ISBN: 978-0-7166-2732-6

Animals at Work
ISBN: 978-0-7166-2724-1 (set, hc)

Also available as:
ISBN: 978-0-7166-2745-6 (e-book)

Printed in China by Shenzhen Wing King Tong Paper Products Co, Ltd., Shenzhen, Guangdong
1st printing August 2018

Staff

Writer: Cath Senker

Executive Committee

President
Jim O'Rourke

Vice President and Editor in Chief
Paul A. Kobasa

Vice President, Finance
Donald D. Keller

Vice President, Marketing
Jean Lin

Vice President, International
Maksim Rutenberg

Vice President, Technology
Jason Dole

Director, Human Resources
Bev Ecker

Editorial

Director, Print Publishing
Tom Evans

Managing Editor
Jeff De La Rosa

Editor
William D. Adams

Manager, Contracts & Compliance
(Rights & Permissions)
Loranne K. Shields

Manager, Indexing Services
David Pofelski

Librarian
S. Thomas Richardson

Digital

Director, Digital Product Development
Erika Meller

Digital Product Manager
Jonathan Wills

Manufacturing/Production

Manufacturing Manager
Anne Fritzinger

Proofreader
Nathalie Strassheim

Graphics and Design

Senior Art Director
Tom Evans

Senior Designer
Don Di Sante

Media Editor
Rosalia Bledsoe

Special thanks to:

Roberta Bailey
Nicola Barber
Francis Paola Lea
Claire Munday
Alex Woolf

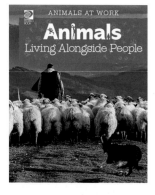

A shepherd and his dog herd sheep in Spain. Both sheep and dogs are very important animals to people.

Acknowledgments

Cover photo: © Jesus Keller, Shutterstock

Alamy: 5 (Images-USA), 6-7 (Stan Gregg), 8-9 (Denis Crawford), 10-11 (Dominic Robinson), 14 (Myrleen Pearson), 17 (EnVogue_Photo), 21 (Tribune Content Agency LLC), 22-23 (David Grossman), 24-25, 28-29 & 32-33 (imageBROKER), 26 (Tony Giammarino), 30-31 (USDA Photo), 39 (SuperStock), 42-43 (BSIP SA).
Shutterstock: title page & 4 (Anirut Thailand), 7 (Juan Gaertner), 8 (majo1122331), 9 (Lorenzo Sala), 10 (Paul Reeves Photography), 12-13 (BunionBear), 13 (Heiko Kiera), 14-15 (Monkey Business Images), 16-17 (NicoleBernardon87), 18 (Mircea Costina), 18-19 (Paul Broadbent), 22 (Vishnevskiy Vasily), 25 & 47 (Erni), 26-27 (Sergei Brik), 28 (GR92100), 33 (gabriel12), 34 (Marin James), 34-35 (PlusONE), 36-37 (frank60), 37 (visualpower), 40-41 (Mary Ann McDonald), 41 (Alexey Seafarer), 43 (Creative Nature Media), 44-45 (Jose Gil).

Contents

4 Introduction

6 Animals in Our Homes

12 Animal Companions

16 Animals in Town

24 Living in Our Wastelands

30 Our Animal Workforce

36 Animals Versus Humans

42 Animal Testing

46 Glossary

47 Find Out More

48 Index

Introduction

Animals and humans are connected in many important ways. Of course, humans are animals, too. We developed from apelike creatures millions of years ago. In prehistoric times, people hunted animals for their meat, hides (skins), and bones. More than 10,000 years ago, humans started to feed and protect some animals that were especially easy to control. These herders only allowed animals with useful traits—such as being calm or producing much meat—to breed (make more animals like themselves). These **domesticated** animals provide humans with everything from transportation to food. Domesticated animals have thrived due to their partnership with humans, while their wild ancestors have mostly disappeared.

For centuries, people have used strong animals, such as oxen, to pull heavy plows to help in farming.

In fact, humans have affected wild animal populations throughout our history. In prehistoric times, it is likely that humans hunted many kinds of large animals to **extinction.** Later, as humans cleared more land for farming and grazing, other wild animals were forced from their **habitats,** causing more **species** to die out. Extinctions continue today as habitats are lost through **climate change** and our overuse of natural resources.

A few kinds of wild animals have benefited from the spread of **agriculture** and human settlements. They may be able to feed in farm fields and **pastures,** live in our homes, or eat our waste. Many have become successful even though humans think they are pests. Many are also **invasive species,** harming **ecosystems** when they arrive.

As humans, we need and use animals in many ways. Most people eat some kinds animals or animal products. Animals work for people in homes and on farms and entertain them in zoos and circuses. Researchers experiment on animals in their efforts to cure disease.

In this book, you will read about the animals that live alongside us, starting with those that share our homes, gardens, and backyards. You will learn about the wildlife in our streets and parks that has successfully adapted to city life.

Zoos allow people to get safely close to wild animals and to learn more about them.

Animals in Our Homes

We share our homes and gardens with a lot of animals. They eat other animals or plants. Some help themselves to our food scraps.

HIDDEN HOUSEMATES

Our animal housemates may arrive by accident, such as on cut flowers; to get away from the cold or heat; or to look for food. Some animals cannot survive indoors, but others do well in buildings. Many are **arthropods,** such as spiders, **insects,** and centipedes. Houses in the United States may contain up to 100 types of arthropods. They can be found in every room of the house. Most do not bother us at all. Arthropods find meals on the floors and surfaces of our homes. Book lice are insects that eat dead insects, mold, and stored food. House centipedes are helpful to humans because they eat pests, such as cockroaches and flies. Silverfish are flat, shiny insects that survive on food with few **nutrients**—and by eating things we would not think of as food. They eat paper, glue, and leather, as well as dead insects and crumbs.

SPIDERS AND BEETLES

Many spiders enjoy the indoor life. Cellar spiders often live in basements, spinning webs to trap small arthropods. They also **scavenge** on insects that could not survive indoors and died once they got inside. Cellar spiders may invade other spiders' webs and steal their **prey,** too. Other creatures go in and out of doors. Ground beetles may enter houses searching for small arthropods to eat, but live outside. Homes with gardens suit their lifestyle perfectly.

Pest guests

Arthropod guests can be troublesome. Dust mites are tiny animals that can cause allergic reactions in some people, making them sneeze, cough, or itch. Flies are common unwelcome guests. They land on uncovered food, spreading germs. In summer, fruit flies feed in our fruit bowls, mosquitoes may bite us, and wasps may sting us.

A magnified view of dust mites in a pillow. The mites live on dead cells that have fallen from human skin.

The common house spider spins webs in houses and other buildings.

HELPERS IN THE GARDEN

Gardens with flowers, fruit, and vegetables attract many small creatures: bees, beetles, worms, spiders, slugs, and snails. Ponds are a home for fish and a breeding ground for such **amphibians** as frogs and salamanders. Many animals are useful to their human neighbors.

Beetles play a valuable part in garden **ecosystems.** They eat the slugs and caterpillars that destroy garden plants, as well as dead plants and animals. Beetles also make holes in rotting wood, helping to break it down and return its **nutrients** to the soil. They are nature's cleaners.

Worms help to keep the soil healthy. They dig down in the earth and make tunnels, which let in water and air. Plant roots can grow in the spaces. Worms make plant food by bringing down leaves and grass from the surface and mixing them with the soil to make it rich with nutrients.

Pests harm garden plants, but other garden visitors may eat the pests. Frogs eat slugs and snails, and ladybugs eat tiny, leaf-eating **insects** called aphids (*AY fihdz, AF ihdz*). Many **species** of bird eat garden pests.

POLLINATORS

Bees, butterflies, moths, and hoverflies **pollinate** the flowers of fruit, vegetables, and crops. Pollinators are drawn to the sweet liquid found in flowers called nectar. The most important pollinators are bees. They collect nectar to make honey, which they use as food. While a bee is collecting nectar from a flower, some of the pollen from the flower sticks to its hairy body. When it visits another flower, the pollen from the bee rubs off on it, enabling the flower to make seeds. The action of pollinators produces about one third of the food we eat.

A pollen-covered bee collects nectar from a dandelion.

Earthworms are covered with a slimy fluid that helps them to move through the soil.

Danger in the compost

Mice and rats may get into compost bins, searching for food. This may seem harmless, but they can carry diseases, such as Lyme disease, in their feces (*FEE seez;* solid wastes). If not treated, Lyme disease can cause joint pain, heart disease, and other problems.

There is lots of food for a rat in this garden compost pile.

FEEDING AROUND OUR HOMES

Foxes, opossums, and raccoons are not picky eaters and are willing to try new things. This makes them well suited to living around us humans. Gray foxes are found in the eastern, north-central, and southwestern United States. Red foxes live throughout most of the United States and nearly all cities in the United Kingdom. Gardens in the suburbs suit foxes well—there are hiding places and lots of food. Foxes can smell food scraps and sift through garbage to find them. They also eat pet food left outdoors. But foxes prefer their natural diet when they can find it. They usually hunt small **mammals,** such as rabbits, mice, and rats, but they sometimes attack chickens and lambs. If they cannot find **prey** to hunt, they will **scavenge** on dead animals.

OPPORTUNITIES FOR OPOSSUMS

Opossums also eat pet food left outdoors, food from the garbage, and birdseed. They may even sleep over at their latest "restaurant," sheltering under a deck or in a garage, or in an attic if they can get in. But they can also help humans. Opossums eat such pests as snails, slugs, **insects,** mice, and rats.

RABBITS ON THE RAMPAGE

Cottontail rabbits live across most of North America. They are major pests in the suburban gardens and parks where they live. In spring and summer, they munch on vegetables, herbs, and flowers. In the fall and winter, they nibble the bark and fruit of shrubs and small trees, making these plants more likely to get diseases and infections.

A cottontail rabbit nibbles on a leaf.

Raccoons: talented thieves

Raccoons are smart mammals with hand-like paws that they use to get at food in hard-to-reach places. They can sneak through pet doors to steal food inside houses. They have become skilled at opening garbage can lids to pick out leftover chicken, fish, and other discarded meals. They can even open hooks, bolts, and latches on doors to reach food.

A red fox searches for food in a dumpster.

Animal Companions

Many people keep tame animals as pets. They provide companionship, relieve stress, and even help people with disabilities. They become members of the family.

FAVORITE PETS

The most common pets include dogs, cats, hamsters, gerbils, rabbits, parakeets, canaries, and fish. Dogs and cats must be trained. Puppies are taught not to urinate or defecate (*YUR uh nayt, DEHF uh kayt;* get rid of liquid and solid wastes) inside the home or chew things in the house. Kittens are trained to use a litterbox. Most dogs have to be taken outside for daily walks.

KEPT IN CAGES

Most other pets are kept in hutches, cages, or tanks. Gerbils, rabbits, and guinea pigs are happier when kept with a companion, but hamsters prefer to be alone. In the wild, most **rodents**—like gerbils—run long distances searching for food, so it is good to take a rodent out of its cage every day for a change of scenery and some exercise. For example, rabbits and guinea pigs enjoy running in a protected outdoor space. Rodents are gnawing animals. They need to gnaw (chew and bite) on wood and other hard things to keep their teeth healthy.

Birds are popular pets, especially in small homes. A birdcage takes up little space, and a pet bird can get good exercise even by flying around a small room. Canaries sing songs, and parakeets learn to talk and copy human voices. Fish are kept in tanks, and people enjoy watching them swim around.

Abandoned snakes

Some people keep wild animals as pets, including snakes. Such pets may grow to large sizes, needing lots of space, food, and care. Owners who no longer want to take care of these pets sometimes release them into the wild. Most released animals die, but some harm the environment. Large numbers of Burmese pythons now live in the Everglades in the southern U.S. state of Florida. They were at first likely abandoned there by pet owners. But due to the warm climate and a lack of natural **predators,** the snakes have reproduced and spread. They are now an **invasive species** there, eating native animals and harming the Everglades **ecosystem.**

A Burmese python in the Everglades. Scientists have had to remove thousands of these snakes to protect the native Everglades animals.

Guinea pigs are rodents that originally came from South America.

PETS: GOOD FOR HEALTH

Pets can be great for people's health. Stroking a cat can help someone to feel calm, and walking a dog is great exercise. Pets also provide a useful connection with the natural world.

It can be valuable for children to have a pet. It helps them learn how to care for another creature and understand its needs: food, water, and a safe place to sleep. Treating animals with patience and kindness teaches children useful skills for dealing with people, too.

A girl feeds her pet cat.

LESSONS FOR LIFE

Having a pet is good for learning about relationships. If an owner is affectionate toward his or her pet, the animal returns the affection. It is an excellent model for forming trusting and loving relationships with people.

Caring for a pet helps people to understand the cycle of life, from growing up to having babies to sickness and death. It helps us learn how to cope with emotions, such as experiencing the loss or death of a pet. These are useful life lessons.

PET THERAPY

Some charities provide **therapy** animals, usually dogs or cats. Owners bring their pets to visit people in nursing homes, hospitals, and prisons. People at these facilities like to cuddle or play with the therapy animals. Some people enjoy simply watching the animals play or perform tricks. Stroking and spending time with a friendly animal can help people feel better. An animal can provide company for isolated people and relieve stress. Some institutions keep cats, birds, or fish so residents can enjoy them every day.

This therapy dog has been trained to provide comfort and affection to people who are ill in hospitals.

Animals in Town

Animals have settled all around our towns and cities. There are fewer dangers from **predators** than in the country and lots of food and shelter. **Insects,** small **rodents,** and **reptiles** make homes in gaps and holes inside buildings, while birds nest in trees and on roofs. Foxes roam the streets and gardens, and water birds settle near ponds and lakes.

PIGEONS EVERYWHERE

Birds called pigeons can be found in cities all over the world. Many kinds of pigeons live alongside us, and several depend on humans for their daily diet. Found throughout Europe, the collared dove eats food scraps and crumbs people drop in the streets. It nests in the gutters of houses and in abandoned buildings. Pigeons are no dirtier than other birds, but their large numbers can cause problems. Huge amounts of droppings fall on the spaces below pigeon nesting areas. In addition to carrying diseases, the droppings can erode (wear away) stone, cause steel to rust, and block drains.

SEAGULLS BY THE SEA

Seagulls are a common sight along coastlines. For some people, these birds are part of the seaside experience, but others find them to be a nuisance. Gulls call noisily, leave droppings everywhere, and boldly search for food. They have become accustomed to human food from leftover snacks that litter the streets and open spaces. When people feed seagulls, they make matters worse. The birds have learned to lurk near humans, looking to be fed, and may even attack them or steal food right out of their hands.

A large group of pigeons rests on top of traffic lights in New York City.

City seagulls

Seagulls have also moved inland. Fish populations have crashed due to overfishing and **climate change,** so some seagulls have wandered into cities in search of a better food supply. They nest on the rooftops of buildings. In cities, they eat scraps from garbage cans, ripping open plastic bags to reach the food waste inside. Human food is bad for seagulls, though. They should be eating fish and **insects,** not half-eaten fries and breadcrumbs.

A seagull pecks at garbage in a city street.

HOUSE MICE

Wild house mice live alongside people all over the world. They have adapted successfully to living in buildings because they need only warmth, shelter, and a little food to survive. They build their nests in houses or garages. Any dark, warm place suits them, including boxes, cupboards, and drawers. Mice have sharp teeth for eating **arthropods** and tough seeds. Those sharp teeth also allow them to tear through food packaging. Mice eat all kinds of human food, especially bread, crackers, and cereal. Mice that get into buildings can be serious pests. In addition to eating food intended for humans, their droppings may contain dangerous diseases (see page 9).

BIGGER BRAINS

Researchers have found that bats, gophers, mice, squirrels, and voles in some cities have bigger brains than their country relatives. They have adapted quickly to their new **habitat,** food sources, and lifestyle, constantly learning new habits and skills that they were not born with. For instance, because cities are so noisy, city squirrels have started to use tail waving instead of sounds to communicate. The growing abilities of these **species** have increased their brain size.

City animals' larger brains enable them to solve more complex problems than country animals. A scientific experiment has shown that city finches have learned how to open the lid or drawer of a semitransparent (partly see-through) plastic box to get to food. Their cousins from the country cannot do this. In another experiment, raccoons had to pull the lid off a garbage can that had been fastened with an elastic cord. None of the country raccoons could do it—but 80 percent of city raccoons could.

Two city-dwelling raccoons search for food in a garbage can.

House mice eat food crumbs and leftovers, but can also tear through food packaging with their sharp front teeth.

Less stressed?

Small **mammals** in city areas show fewer signs of stress than country ones when they are surprised or threatened. It could be that they no longer react as strongly to such surprising events because of the constant noise and traffic of the city. If they became anxious every time a vehicle passed or somebody shouted, it would be hard to survive.

City Coyotes

Coyotes are medium-sized, wolf-like animals that used to live only in southwestern North America. Ranchers in the western United States hated coyotes, wrongly blaming them for killing **livestock** and wild animals that could be hunted. From the 1930's to the 1970's, the U.S. government tried to wipe out the coyote, poisoning and shooting them in the millions. Coyotes managed not only to survive, but also to spread throughout the country. Many have done well living near people.

Like many animals that have moved to areas where people live, coyotes prefer the suburbs. Large residential lots, empty farm fields, and forest preserves give coyotes lots of land in which to hunt. But coyotes must cross all kinds of roads, from sleepy cul-du-sacs to busy highways, to use this space. Coyotes watch for traffic and time their crossings to stoplights, but many are still killed in collisions with vehicles.

In some places, coyotes have moved all the way into cities. Researchers estimate that some 2,000 coyotes have settled inside the city limits of Chicago, a large city of the central United States. These coyotes have larger home **ranges** than suburban ones because some areas, such as busy streets, cannot be used. The coyotes eat their natural foods when they can, hunting such

prey as rabbits and birds that have also moved into the city. If they cannot find such prey, they make do with **insects,** fruit, and people's leftover food. One coyote in Chicago was found to eat food that mourners placed on their loved ones' graves in a cemetery.

While most coyotes move about during the day, city and suburban coyotes have become mostly **nocturnal** to avoid their human neighbors. Sometimes, though, these coyotes attack pets and— very rarely—people. Wildlife researchers point out that humans often bring about such attacks. For example, someone might feed a coyote, causing it to lose its fear of people over time and attack someone else in the area.

A COYOTE on a sidewalk in Chicago. Coyotes build hidden dens to sleep in during the day—often just a few feet or a meter or two away from homes, sidewalks, and storefronts.

PARK LIFE

Parks are perfect homes for many city-dwelling animals, offering them natural areas with trees, plants, and water. Many different **mammals,** birds, fish and **arthropods** are found in parks.

New York City parks are home to bats, coyotes, opossums, red foxes, skunks, squirrels, and white-tailed deer. At night, skunks and bats come out to eat. Skunks spray a foul substance to put off **predators,** and they look for food at night to avoid them, too. Opossums are also **nocturnal.** They find ready-made shelters in hollowed logs or piles of branches. Squirrels live in the trees, eating nuts, berries, and seeds. People sometimes feed squirrels, but it is better for them to find their own food. The squirrels bury their food supplies in the fall to last them through the winter. Skunks and bats avoid the seasonal food shortage by **hibernating** through the cold New York winter from October to April.

A squirrel takes food that has been left on a feeder in a city park.

PONDS AND LAKES

Water birds feed in and around ponds and lakes, and nest on their shores. Ducks, geese, and swans eat tiny animals floating in the water and plants, including grass and seaweed. Some ducks have a broad bill with many tiny filters along the edges. They take large mouthfuls of water, and the filters trap food, allowing the water to drain away. Other ducks, and other birds, including herons and terns, have long, pointed bills with sharp edges for catching fish. Migrating birds use ponds and lakes as a place to rest and eat before continuing their journeys.

Swans, geese, and ducks share the icy waters of a lake in Prospect Park, in New York City, after a snowstorm.

Living in Our Wastelands

Some animals driven out of their natural **habitats** have adapted to live in places most people avoid. Some search for food at landfills. Our sewers (underground drains) are home to huge rat populations.

THE LANDFILL HABITAT

In many places, garbage is buried in landfills, which are filled and then sealed. As landfills are filling up, many animals feed at them. In other areas, garbage is simply thrown into open dumps, which animals can get to even more easily. These dumps are full of life.

At landfills and dumps, cockroaches and ants eat rotting waste. Mice, voles, and other small **mammals** dig to find food. Raccoons, coyotes, and dogs search the surface. From the air, crows, starlings, and gulls fly in to feed. They themselves can be eaten by birds of prey. Rats and other **omnivores** do best at landfills and dumps. They can make use of the wide variety of food available there. Rats will even eat dog feces. Large animals, including bears and baboons in Africa and the Arabian Peninsula, also visit landfills to feed. At some landfills, the bears are no longer scared of the garbage trucks, and even eat while the trucks are dumping waste.

FOOD WEBS

A complex food web—what eats what—has formed at landfills. **Rodents** eat small creatures and leftover food. In turn, the rodents are eaten by coyotes, foxes, and snakes. Spiders eat flies and other **arthropods,** which are all **prey** for small birds. Larger birds of prey, such as eagles, eat these birds.

A grizzly bear searches for food in a landfill in the far northwestern U.S. state of Alaska.

Life-saving landfills

Landfills are helping some **endangered** animals to survive. An example is the Egyptian vulture, a large **scavenging** bird found in parts of Europe, Africa, the Middle East, and India. The population in Europe has shrunk rapidly over the past 20 years. But in Spain, numbers of the birds nesting close to landfills climbed between 1988 and 2014.

An Egyptian vulture in flight in Spain.

JUNK FOOD

Animals eat junk food at landfills. The food is plentiful, but it is less nutritious than an animal's natural diet, so the animal needs to eat more of it to survive. Such junk food is especially bad for birds, which already must eat large amounts to fuel their high **metabolisms.** As they struggle to fill up at landfills, they also end up eating things that are not food, such as plastic. In turn, birds of prey eat those birds, which are literally full of garbage.

Animals can also eat human foods that are poisonous to them. In one incident, gulls died after eating chocolate at a landfill in Vancouver, Canada. Chocolate is safe for people to eat, but it contains chemicals that are poisonous to many other animals. Even if such poisons do not kill an animal, they can make it sick and unhealthy. Like humans, unhealthy creatures are more likely to suffer **organ** failure and cancer.

STORKS' STAYCATION

Storks usually fly south from Europe and Asia to spend the winter in South Africa. Before the 1980's, all the storks in Portugal migrated. Scientists have noticed that some storks now stay in Portugal. By 2016, 80 percent of the storks that stayed in Portugal over the winter stayed at open garbage dumps. If these open-air trash pits are closed up, it could push the storks to start migrating again.

FED ON FOOD WASTE

Some food waste can be used to feed **domesticated** animals. This way, companies avoid the cost of disposing it in a landfill, and farmers save money because food scraps are cheaper to buy than animal feed. Some states in the United States allow this trade. To prevent health problems, governments regulate what kinds of food can be collected. For example, no meat or dairy products are allowed. Rutgers University in New Jersey collects food waste from its dining halls to feed to the hogs and cattle at a local farm. It costs the university half as much as sending the waste to a landfill.

A farmer feeds his pigs. Pigs can eat human food scraps.

A flock of black storks begins its long migration from Europe to spend the winter in South Africa.

SEWER RATS

Rats live on every continent except Antarctica. They are perfectly suited to life in the sewers—in fact, another name for the brown rat is "sewer rat." Originally introduced from Europe on ships, brown rats can now be found in cities all over the world.

Rats have several traits that allow them to do well in the sewers. They are **nocturnal** and do not rely much on their eyesight, so the darkness does not slow them down like it would other animals. Rats are smart and are strong swimmers. These traits help them get around in complex sewer networks. They have a strong sense of smell that helps them to find food, and can dig and gnaw through most materials to go where they want.

STUCK DOWN THE SEWER

Some animals make short journeys into the sewers. Stray dogs and cats may use drainage pipes and sewers as shelter. Such **predators** as snakes may follow rats and mice into the sewers, looking for a meal. But the challenging conditions of sewers keep most animals from living there for a long time. Animals can get trapped in sewers, however.

Though alligators have never colonized the sewers of New York City, as claimed in urban legends, they do sometimes get stuck in sewers in their home **range** in Florida. Animals as large as cows have been trapped down drains, too.

An iguana emerges from a sewer in Costa Rica.

In 2016, rats surged out of the sewers in Paris, France, in large numbers, coming out into parks and gardens to eat garbage. City officials had to close several parks. Workers sealed the sewer entrances to stop the rats from getting out again. It was an unusual incident: sewer rats usually stay in their damp, smelly underground hideouts.

A brown rat pops out from a city drain cover at night.

Our Animal Workforce

People keep animals to provide food and clothing and to help them in different ways. Many kinds of animals entertain people in safari parks, zoos, and at the races

SNIFFER DOGS

Dogs have a powerful sense of smell. Sniffer dogs are trained to sense many substances, including illegal drugs, firearms, currency, and explosives. To train them, handlers reward them with a treat or by playing with them each time they correctly identify a targeted scent. The dogs work at airports to check for any passengers trying to take banned items on a flight. At music festivals or other public gatherings, they check people for drugs and weapons. The police sometimes use dogs to find missing people and track criminals through their scent.

SERVICE DOGS

Some dogs are specially trained to help people with disabilities. A guide dog helps a person who is blind or has trouble seeing to safely navigate through his or her community. A hearing dog can let someone with a hearing impairment know about different sounds around the house, such as telephone calls, knocks at the door, or alarms. A mobility assistance dog helps its owner to pick up objects, get dressed and undressed, and to go up and down stairs. Dogs can even be trained to sense if their owner is about to get sick and let them know so the person can take action or move to a safe place.

A sniffer dog at Washington Dulles International Airport shows its handler that it has smelled an illegal substance in luggage.

Guard dogs

Some people keep dogs to guard their homes and businesses. Often, a dog is enough to drive away a would-be thief. Even if the dog is small, its barking can tell people nearby that something is wrong. Some dogs will attack intruders. Specially trained attack dogs often serve in police departments and militaries. Such dogs may also be trained to sense weapons, such as explosives.

ON THE FARM

Farm animals provide people with many products, including eggs, hides, meat, milk, and wool. Some farmers keep bees to **pollinate** their crops and to make honey. Children raised on family farms may learn to care for the animals. They may milk the cows or goats, feed the animals, and collect eggs. Sometimes they have pet lambs, rabbits, and piglets, and may learn to ride horses.

Some farmers keep animals to work, too. Dogs herd sheep and cattle to stop them from straying and to protect them from **predators.** Cats hunt mice and rats. Some animals are of great value for their strength. In many parts of the world, farmers use donkeys, mules, oxen, horses, or camels to pull plows and move goods.

FACTORY FARMS

Many animals are raised in large factory farms. It is especially common for **livestock** farmers to raise chickens and pigs in a building and to keep them from going outside. Many processes are automated in factory farms, such as the feeding of animals and the removal of their wastes. Operators of small farms have difficulty competing in the livestock market with factory farms.

Some people claim that there are problems with factory farming. They are concerned that animal wastes from large farms are polluting the nearby land and water. Also, they believe that animals in factory farms are abused and diseased. But other people say that factory farms are clean and healthy. They point out that poor conditions lead to animals being sick, small, or unable to reproduce, resulting in no profit for the farm operators

THE NOMADIC LIFE

Some farmers travel with their animals over many miles or kilometers, living a nomadic lifestyle. Nomads move around with their camels, cattle, goats, sheep, or yaks to find water and **pastures** to graze. The Fulani keep cattle in the grasslands of Niger, in western Africa. The Bedouin travel through the deserts of the Arabian Peninsula with camels, goats, and sheep. But this lifestyle is becoming rare. Pastures are often turned into cropland, forcing nomads to move to towns and cities.

Speedy species

Horses and greyhounds can run fast, and some are specially trained to sprint around a track. Some horses become famous for their racing abilities. Gamblers bet on which animal will win the race. Racing is a big, profitable business.

A racehorse is urged on by its jockey (rider).

A rancher rides a horse to herd her cattle in the northwestern U.S. state of Oregon.

ZOOS AND SAFARI PARKS

People love to see animals from around the world. Most large cities have a zoo. Some have creatures from across the globe, while smaller ones may keep one type of animal, such as birds or monkeys. Aquariums have fish and other aquatic animals on show. Zoo animals live in cages, tanks, and enclosures filled with the natural features of their wild **habitat,** such as trees and ponds.

In safari parks, such as Masai Mara in East Africa, the wildlife roams freely. People view the animals from vehicles. The San Diego Zoo Safari Park in California has antelope, giraffes, lions, rhinoceroses, and zebras. Visitors watch them from a train that runs through the park.

A magnificent lion at San Diego Zoo Safari Park

SAVING SPECIES

Zoos are important refuges for **endangered species.** They run breeding programs, bringing together pairs of animals so that they can reproduce. Such breeding programs have helped to save some species from **extinction,** such as the European bison and the Arabian oryx. Zoos are also involved in education. Exhibits teach people about the natural world and environmental problems that affect animals. They may host programs that teach children about caring for zoo animals.

People can view ocean life through an underwater tunnel at the Dubai Aquarium, in the United Arab Emirates.

The circus debate

Many circuses feature trained animals. Chimpanzees ride bicycles, dogs jump rope, and tigers leap through hoops of fire. Some countries allow only **domesticated** animals to be in circuses. In others, trained wild animals, such as elephants and lions, are allowed. Some people campaign against using any animals at the circus. They claim the creatures are worked too hard, are kept in small spaces, and have to travel often, with little chance to exercise. But circus supporters claim they treat the animals well and give them a healthy living environment.

Animals Versus Humans

People and animals do not always get along well. Pests ruin crops, some animals carry diseases that affect humans, and a few creatures even kill people. In turn, humans have a devastating effect on the animal world

RATS: DAMAGE AND DISEASE

On farms, rats eat stored grains, fruits, and vegetables and may attack chickens, piglets, and lambs. If they get into houses, they gnaw pipes and furniture, causing serious problems. These **rodents** can even cause fires if they chew into electric wires. Rats carry the germs of dangerous diseases that they can spread to humans. To reduce rat numbers, people poison, shoot, or trap them. Pest controllers treat food with special drugs to stop rats from reproducing

DEADLY INSECTS

The deadliest animal to humans is the tiny mosquito. Some mosquitoes carry a disease called malaria that kills millions of people every year in Africa and Southeast Asia. Another mosquito carries the Zika virus, which causes birth defects in the children of infected mothers. The tsetse fly of **sub-Saharan Africa** is extremely harmful, too. It spreads sleeping sickness, which kills around 10,000 people every year.

RABID ATTACKERS

Rabies is a disease that destroys the nerve cells of part of the brain and nearly always kills its victim. Animals that are infected with rabies are said to be rabid. Rabid dogs, cats, and wild animals often become aggressive and will bite a person without reason, infecting them with the disease. The person will die if he or she is not treated right away.

Locusts

A locust is a type of grasshopper. Locusts can form huge **swarms** of billions of **insects,** which travel to find food. These swarms eat all kinds of plants and wipe out entire crops. They can even make transportation dangerous. Huge swarms can block out the sun, making it hard to see. Bodies of locusts can clog aircraft engines and make roads and rails slick. To prevent locust swarms, farmers plow the soil in the late fall to kill the eggs or poison the locusts soon after they hatch.

A locust is a type of grasshopper.

The Aedes mosquito carries the Zika virus, which is especially dangerous to pregnant women.

Snakes

A few animals, such as crocodiles, elephants, hippopotamuses, and lions, sometimes kill humans. Many people believe sharks to be dangerous killers, but they only kill about 10 people each year. Apart from disease-spreading animals, such as mosquitoes and rabid dogs, snakes are the deadliest animals to humans.

Snakes usually try to avoid people. If a **venomous** snake is threatened or surprised, it will often warn the intruder. A rattlesnake makes a rattling sound with the tip of its tail. A cobra flattens out its neck, revealing a flashy hood. Others may open their mouths wide, showing fangs or warning colors. A venomous snake will usually only attack if the intruder does not heed its warning. If you see a snake, especially one showing some sort of warning, it is best to stand still or back away slowly.

Even though many venomous snakes give these warnings, millions of people are still bitten each year. Some venomous snakes like to live in places where people are around, such as farm fields or warm houses. Someone may not notice a snake, or even step on it. Snakebite kills at least 20,000 and as many as 125,000 people every year, and disables many more.

People in poorer countries are far more likely to be affected by snakebite. Richer countries, such as Australia and the United States, have many **species** of venomous snakes. But very few people die from snakebite in those countries because they have strong medical systems that can quickly treat victims. In many parts of Africa and Asia, people may have to travel for hours to reach the nearest hospital. Even then, the hospital might not have the right **antivenom.** A single type of antivenom does not work against bites from all species of snake, so hospitals must stock many different kinds. Some drug companies have even stopped making antivenoms because selling them does not make the companies much money. But a few companies are creating new antivenoms that can work against many kinds of snake **venom.** If such new antivenoms are cheap and easy to store, they could save many thousands of lives each year.

The RUSSELL'S VIPER, found throughout India and southeast Asia, is one of the deadliest of all the venomous snakes.

DESTROYING THE RAIN FORESTS

We are harming our animal neighbors, destroying their **habitats** through industry, **agriculture,** and **climate change.** People clear rain forests to provide wood and make space for farms and towns. Each year, up to 40 million acres (16 million hectares) of tropical forests are lost. The rain forests are rich in plant and animal life, containing more **species** per square yard or meter than any other habitat.

Many rain forest species are **endangered.** The mountain gorillas of eastern Zaire, Rwanda, and Uganda in eastern Africa depend on the leaves, stems, and fruit of such plants as bamboo. They are threatened because of the destruction of their forest habitat and hunting

OVERFISHING

Most fish reproduce quickly, so when an adult is caught, there are many young fish to replace it. But today, more than 85 percent of the world's fisheries are overfished. So many fish are caught each year at these places that there are not enough left to breed and replace the fish stocks. The result is that there are fewer fish to catch each year. Some species that many people like to eat have become endangered, such as the Atlantic bluefin tuna.

HABITAT LOSS

Global warming is making many parts of the world hotter and drier, and the overuse of land makes the problem worse. In Africa, the Sahara is spreading south. There are too many **livestock** animals grazing and trampling the soil and people chopping down trees for firewood. Wild animals are losing their habitat, and their food supplies are declining because of competition from livestock.

Shrinking sea ice

In the Arctic, polar bears breed on the sea ice and rest there during their hunts for seals. Global warming is causing the sea ice to melt. Over the last 20 years, it has been shrinking at a faster rate than ever before. Polar bears are more likely to become exhausted and drown without sea ice on which they can rest.

Female polar bears raising young cubs are at greatest risk of starvation.

Animal Testing

Animals are used for testing drugs and other products because they have many **organ** systems and body processes like those of humans. Experiments may involve **amphibians,** fish, and **insects.** Scientists also use different birds and **mammals,** including monkeys, mice, and rats.

WHY EXPERIMENT ON ANIMALS?

Tests on animals can help scientists to learn more about how the human body works. Researchers study animal behavior to see how creatures learn and how memory functions, which helps them understand how the human brain works. They can find out the causes of serious illnesses, such as heart disease and cancer. Scientists check how surgeries affect animals before trying them out on humans. Surgical methods, such as joint replacement and heart surgery, were practiced on animals before they were tried on humans. Ways to diagnose diseases, including CT and MRI scans, were also first tested on animals.

Animal experimentation is an important step in the process of creating new drugs. Companies test drugs on animals to see if they do what they are supposed to do. They also use such tests to learn if a drug is safe or has any side effects. Companies will only test a drug on people if it has proven to be safe and effective in animals

OUR SHARED GENES

It might seem strange that these experiments can help researchers because people seem to be so different from animals. But we are not that different. We share most of our **genes** with mice and suffer from some of the same illnesses, such as cancers and heart disease. People also share genes with **domesticated** animals and give them medicines like the ones we use ourselves, including painkillers and **antibiotics.**

Veterinary science

Animal testing can benefit animals, too. Veterinarians use the results of animal testing to help treat pets. This research is also important for farm animals. Animals are often kept close together on farms, so any outbreak of disease can quickly infect many individuals. Antibiotics and **vaccines** developed through animal testing can help to prevent the spread of disease, saving animals' lives.

In farms where cows or other farm animals are kept close together, disease can spread quickly.

While mice and rats are the most common laboratory animals, insects and other creatures are also used for research.

AGAINST ANIMAL TESTING

Some people oppose animal testing of any kind. They argue that it is wrong to sicken or kill animals on purpose. They also say that the experiments may not provide useful results for humans because animals are not the same as us. Opponents say that experiments could be carried out using **bacteria** or pieces of human or animal **tissue,** without killing any animals. Computer models could be used, too.

Many animal experiments are performed for medical reasons. But animals are also used to test the safety of substances added to food and beauty products. Some people believe it is acceptable to use animals for medical research, but not for testing such commercial products.

SCIENTIFIC PROGRESS

Most scientists think it is useful to experiment on animals to make progress in science. They argue that researchers need to know how a drug affects the body as a whole, not just a piece of tissue. Some animals are harmed, but there are huge benefits to humankind. They point to the many **vaccines** and medications created with the help of animal testing and to the many millions of human lives such treatments have saved. They believe experimentation should continue because it will help to save more lives in the future.

THE THREE R'S

Most laboratories try to follow the "three R's" when conducting animal research:

- Reduction: Use as few animals as possible
- Refinement: Minimize distress and pain caused to the animals
- Replacement: Use alternatives to animal testing where possible

Many countries also have laws to enforce these principles. By following the three R's, researchers reduce animal suffering while still enabling society to benefit from animal testing.

Animal testing provokes strong feelings in both its supporters and opponents. These marchers are showing their support of animal testing in medical research.

Alternatives to animal experiments

Medical schools used to use live animals to teach surgery skills to students. In 2016, the last U.S. medical school to use live animals announced it would no longer do so. A better alternative had been created: a computer simulation of the human body that has lifelike **organs** and mimics body functions, such as breathing and bleeding.

Glossary

agriculture the raising of plants and animals for human benefit.

amphibian a vertebrate with scaleless skin that usually lives part of its life in water and part on land. Vertebrate animals have a backbone.

antibiotic a drug containing or using a substance that can destroy or prevent the growth of bacteria and cure infections.

antivenom a drug that can stop and reverse the effects of a particular venom.

arthropod a very large group of invertebrates that includes insects, arachnids, and crustaceans. Invertebrate animals do not have backbones.

bacterium (plural bacteria) a single-celled living thing. Some bacteria can cause disease.

climate change a change in the usual weather of a particular place, often associated with global warming.

domesticate to tame a wild animal over generations to become used to living with or working for humans.

ecosystem a system made up of a group of living things and its physical environment, and the relationship between them.

endangered a species or other group of living thing that is at risk of going extinct.

extinction when every member of a species (kind) of living thing has died.

gene the unit of inheritance, held in living cells. In most animals, parents' genes are combined in their offspring through sexual reproduction.

global warming a worldwide rise in temperatures, caused by air pollution.

habitat the place where a living thing usually makes its home.

hibernate to spend the winter in a state like deep sleep. Breathing, heart rate, and other body processes slow down.

insect one of the major invertebrate groups. Invertebrate animals do not have a backbone. Insects have six legs and a three-part body.

invasive species a type of living thing that spreads rapidly in a new environment where there are few or no natural controls on its growth.

livestock the animals farmers keep for their meat, milk, hides, or wool, such as sheep and goats.

mammal one of the major vertebrate animal groups. Mammals feed their offspring on milk produced by the mother, and most have hair or fur.

metabolism the chemical processes that happen within a living thing to keep it alive.

nocturnal active at night.

nutrient a substance that is needed to keep a living thing alive and help it grow.

omnivore an animal that eats plants and animals.

organ a part of the body, made of similar cells and cell tissue, that performs a particular function.

pasture land covered with grass that is suitable for feeding animals.

pollinate to put pollen into a flower or plant so that it produces seeds.

predator an animal that hunts, kills, and eats other animals.

prey an animal that is hunted, killed, and eaten by another.

range the area in which a species can be found.

reptile one of the major vertebrate animal groups. Vertebrate animals have a backbone. A reptile has dry, scaly skin and breathes air. Snakes, crocodiles, and lizards are all reptiles.

rodent a mammal with front teeth made for gnawing hard things.

scavenge to feed on the carcasses of dead

animals.

species a group of living things that have certain permanent traits in common and are able to reproduce with each other.

sub-Saharan Africa the part of Africa south of the Sahara Desert.

swarm a large group of arthropods moving together either in search of food or a new home.

therapy treatment for a problem or illness.

tissue the material of which living things are made.

vaccine a mild form of a disease, given to protect people or animals from catching the disease in future.

venom a naturally produced liquid that animals can introduce into other animals (for example, through biting) in order to stun, injure, or kill the other animal.

venomous describes an animal that produces venom or a part of such an animal that releases venom.

BOOKS

125 True Stories of Amazing Pets: Inspiring Tales of Animal Friendship and Four-legged Heroes, Plus Crazy Animal Antics by National Geographic Kids (National Geographic Children's Books, 2014)

Barnyard Kids: A Family Guide for Raising Animals by Dina Rudick (Quarry Books, 2015)

City Critters: Wildlife in the Urban Jungle by Nicholas Read (Orca Book Publishers, 2012)

Zoology for Kids: Understanding and Working with Animals, with 21 Activities by Josh Hestermann and Bethanie Hestermann (Chicago Review Press, 2015)

WEBSITES

Compassion in World Farming
https://www.ciwf.com/farm-animals/
Animals we farm and their lives under different farming systems.

Discovery Kids Animals
http://discoverykids.com/category/animals/
Includes animals that live alongside people, such as mosquitos, skunks, and alligators.

Urban Coyote Research Project
https://urbancoyoteresearch.com/
Describes the study of coyotes living in Cook County, Illinois.

alligators 28
animal testing 4, 42–45
aquariums 34–35
Arabian oryx 34

baboons 24
bats 18, 22
bears 24–25, 41
bees 8, 32
beetles 6, 8
birds 8, 12, 14, 16, 20, 22–23, 24, 25, 26–27, 34, 42
butterflies 8

camels 32
canaries 12
cats 12, 14, 28, 32, 36
cattle 26, 32–33, 43
centipedes 6
chickens 10, 32, 36
chimpanzees 35
circuses 4, 35
climate change 4, 17, 40–41
cockroaches 6, 24
coyotes 20–21, 22, 24
crocodiles 38

deer 22
diseases 4, 9, 10, 16, 18, 32, 36, 38, 42, 43
dogs 12, 14–15, 24, 28, 30–31, 32, 35, 36, 38
domesticated animals 4, 26, 32, 35, 42
ducks 22–23
dust mites 7

eagles 24
elephants 35, 38

endangered species 25, 34, 40
European bison 34

farms 4, 20, 26, 32, 36, 38, 40, 43
finches 18
fish 8, 12, 14, 17, 22, 34–35, 40, 42
flies 6, 7, 8, 24, 36
foxes 10–11, 16, 22, 24
frogs 8

geese 22–23
gerbils 12
global warming 40–41
goats 32
gophers 18
gorillas 40–41
greyhounds 33
guinea pigs 12-13

hamsters 12
herons 22
hippopotamuses 38
horses 32–33

iguanas 28
insects 6–7, 8, 10, 16, 17, 20, 36–37, 42–43

ladybugs 8
landfill sites 24–25, 26
lice 6
lions 34, 35, 38
locusts 37

mice 9, 10, 18–19, 24, 28, 32, 42, 43
monkeys 42
mosquitoes 7, 36–37

opossums 10, 22
oxen 4

parakeets 12
parks 22–23, 29
pests 4, 6, 7, 8, 10, 36–37
pets 12–15, 18, 21, 43
pigeons 16–17
pigs 26, 32
polar bears 41

rabbits 10, 12, 20, 32
raccoons 10, 11, 18, 19, 24
rats 9, 10, 24, 28–29, 32, 36, 42, 43

safari parks 30, 34
salamanders 8
seagulls 16, 17, 24, 26
sewers 24, 28, 29
sheep 32
silverfish 6
skunks 22
slugs 8, 10
snails 8, 10
snakes 13, 24, 28, 38–39
spiders 6–7, 8, 24
squirrels 18, 22
storks 26–27
swans 22–23

therapy animals 14–15
tigers 35

voles 18, 24
vultures 25

worms 8–9

zoos 4, 5, 30, 34